Critics on V

"Of some two thousand plu[...] presented Walter Bargen's work more times than any other. *My Other Mother's Red Mercedes* exemplifies why. Here is a poet whose every word is crafted with the precision of a master watchmaker. Describing his mother's survival in Germany in the aftermath of WWII: "Maybe you had to be there/ in the rubble and rape of it all." So many poets hold their work at arm's length distance, or more. Bargen is intimate with his characters and nature without a scintilla of sentimentality. His powers of observation, of both the seen and unseen worlds, is unsurpassed. In *My Other Mother's Red Mercedes*, he occupies his place at the peak of America's most gifted poets."

—Robert Nazarene, founding editor, *The American Journal of Poetry*

"Walter Bargen still understands the art of dedication, something abundantly clear in his latest collection of poetry *Too Quick for the Living* (Moon City Press). In a more exterior way, Bargen uses pen and paper to scrawl the names of friends and comrades at the bottom of many works in this volume. These works are for them as much or more as they are for us, the reader."

—*The Columbia Daily Tribune*

"Bargen's poetry will appeal to anyone who is looking for an elegant, direct poetic examination of the human condition."

—*Foreword Review*

My Other Mother's Red Mercedes

My Other Mother's Red Mercedes

Walter Bargen

LITERARY PRESS
LAMAR UNIVERSITY

ISBN: 978-1-942956-61-7
Library of Congress Control Number: 2018955002

Cover Art Concept: "The Last Kiss" by Nawalahh

Lamar University Literary Press
Beaumont, Texas

Acknowledgments

I am grateful to the editors of the following magazines where some of the poems in this collection originally appeared:

American Journal of Poetry
BoomerLit Magazine
Burningwood Literary Journal
The Cape Rock
Miramar
Penn Review

The poem "Exorcism of the First Spoon" appeared in the book *The Feast* (BkMk Press-UMKC, 2004).

I would like to thank Dr. Tom Dillingham and Matt Dube for their patience in the reading of this manuscript.

I would also like to thank Lynne Jenkins-Lempe, Lois Long, and Zak Wardell for reading early versions of these poems.

Recent Poetry from Lamar University Literary Press

Bobby Aldridge, *An Affair of the Stilled Heart*
Michael Baldwin, *Lone Star Heart, Poems of a Life in Texas*
Roberto Bonazzi, *Awakened by Surprise*
David Bowles, *Flower, Song, Dance: Aztec and Mayan Poetry*
Jerry Bradley and Ulf Kirchdorfer, editors, *The Great American Wise Ass Poetry Anthology*
Jerry Bradley, *Crownfeathers and Effigies*
Matthew Brennan, *One Life*
Mark Busby, *Through Our Times*
Paul Christensen, *The Jack of Diamonds Is a Hard Card to Play*
Stan Crawford, *Resisting Gravity*
Chip Dameron, *Waiting for an Etcher*
Glover Davis, *My Cap of Darkness*
William Virgil Davis, *The Bones Poems*
Jeffrey DeLotto, *Voices Writ in Sand*
Chris Ellery, *Elder Tree*
Alan Gann, *That's Entertainment*
Larry Griffin, *Cedar Plums*
Michelle Hartman, *Irony and Irrelevance*
Ulf Kirchdorfer, *Chewing Green Leaves*
J. Pittman McGehee, *Nod of Knowing*
Jim McGarrah, *A Balancing Act*
Laurence Musgrove, *One Kind of Recording*
Godspower Oboido, *Wandering Feet on Pebbled Shores*
Carol Coffee Reposa, *Underground Musicians*
Jan Seale, *The Parkinson Poems*
Steven Schroeder, *the moon, not the finger, pointing*
Vincent Spina, *The Sumptuous Hills of Gulfport*
W.K. Stratton, *Ranchero Ford/ Dying in Red Dirt Country*
Wally Swist, *Invocation*
Loretta Diane Walker, *Desert Light*
Dan Williams, *Past Purgatory, a Distant Paradise*

For information on these and other Lamar University Literary Press books go to www.Lamar.edu/literarypress

For my mother, Anna Franziska Mader-Bargen (1922-2015)
For my father, M/Sgt William John Bargen (1924-1984)

A Long, Long Way to Go

1

For I have eaten ashes like bread
And mingled my drink with weeping.
                    Psalm 99

2

Children picking our bones
Will never know that these were once
As quick as foxes on the hill.
                    Wallace Stevens

3

She'll be better when she's worse.
                    Gillian Hamilton

4

Your mother should know
Though she was born a long, long time ago
Your mother should know
                    Lennon/McCartney

CONTENTS

I.

Autumn Forests of Yushan

—scroll painting by Wang Hui (1668)

1

Rain beyond rain.
Crickets sing beyond crickets.
Who listens this far?

2

One way.
One way.
No turning back.

3

Handfuls of earth—
This stepping away.
Dust clings.

4

The day cloudy.
Shoes insist we keep walking.
Each step unfathomable.

Limbo

All day in their chairs sphinx-like. The answers
gone before the riddle arrives.

All day their heads bowed, chin to chest. Looking down
   and down.

All day their necks bent back, their mouths open.
   Hatchlings feeding on time's rain.

All day eyes wide, set against pastel walls.
   Horizons mummified.

All day working at discovering another breath
   in their bodies and then its exile.

All day stoic in preparation for the exclamation
   that startles some other lifetime's exclamation.

All day repeating the questions.
   Asking and forgetting the same thing.

Marching Orders

Driving the cemetery road by the river,
it winds into other lifetimes: the tightly lined,
strictly measured stones engraved with the regulation
birth, death, rank, branch of service, and wars,
held within official-sized plots. The mown
grass without a blade out of place.

Thousands of little flags ripped full face to attention
by the parading prairie winds, as if the platoon,
company, battalion, is ready for orders to proceed
to the next objective, which cannot be found
in this place, even though the centuries-old
brass cannons on their spoke-wheeled carriages
all point over the valley at the advancing river currents.
Orders are to "Hold at all costs," reinforcements on the way,
but time's frontal assault is already upon them.

Schuhplattler

Whether on the south-side porch of the house
or where the oaks lean to touch in the yard,
my mother and I are desperate to understand
a life that moves beyond itself,

or on the park ridge where we park and the wind
turns our clothes into kites held by the thin frames
of our bodies blowing beyond us as we search
the wintered fields, for what, we aren't sure,

or in her kitchen after a long drive that settles
nothing, where the dust on a window sill
is a mistake and afraid of the consequences.
She asks month after month

if I have found my father's shoes
those spit-shined black leather ones that lace
up the side, worn by traditional German dancers.
They were not among the shoes

and boots that I took for myself or left
for the Salvation Army.
No, I didn't throw them out.
Yes, I did keep the fur-lined boots.

No, the dance shoes were not there.
Yes, I will keep an eye out for them.
I know they aren't lost.
I want to say, they are something

he took in case he needed to slap
his heels and thighs in light
too bright to take another step
yet must leap . . .

In a moment centuries of June
—Emily Dickinson

We are still in the 14th century, afraid of falling
off the edge of the flat world or into a dank basement.
The maps bordered with mermaids and serpents.
What would my father say?

The file cabinets in the basement empty.
The basement walls repaired and stuccoed to cover
the cracks from the weight of an overeager earth.
The concrete floor practicing the dance called tectonic slippage.

Nothing to be done. The basement on to the next owner.
What would my father say? Papers stored
in a rental unit stolen along with his ice skates
and an eighty year-old baseball catcher's mitt.

Mostly decades of payments, outdated insurance policies,
and a speeding ticket. A measure of the passing
and a small sense of sustaining some order. Maybe electrical
surges and water leakage enough to drown in

but not to launch a ship through these records of payment,
or maybe it's a remembrance, sitting at one end of the sofa
under a lamp reading nothing more than the next round of bills
while listening to the baseball game on the radio

or better watching a pitcher scratch his crotch on TV.
Always the Reds, always loyal to his so-long-ago
hometown team. What would my father say?
How could I claim to know after all these years of silence?

Years and silence not enough to clear up anything.
My father condemned to secrecy, to going darkly medieval.
I'm condemned to put words in his mouth.
What would my father say back in the 14th century?

Amphibious Fear

When my father started marching all
day for months in one place, in line
with other soldiers who can only be
identified with a map that plots out
the rolling hills, ever present for
the growing roll call of gray stones,
my mother tore out walls in their house

and covered the rest with new wallpaper.
One wall of the hallway by the main door
and one by the kitchen, gone, so the living-
room was no longer alone, but entered into
the whole house even as the foundation
shifted and cracked from hydraulic pressure:
the basement floor lifting snapped tiles,

and hairline fissures spread across
the living room ceiling. Bricks started
to loosen and windows no longer opened
or closed. But behind the glass doors of
the kitchen cabinets, at the front edge of
a shelf, backed by violet and vined china,
cut glass and crystal, and painted porcelain

figurines, was a raw pink frog, its mouth
open wide as its body. There is nothing
inside this cavity except the shape of its pimpled
outside gulping a pond-sucking void.
I am afraid to ask its story, why it is there,
surrounded by so much delicate pretension,
and how I must have played with it decades ago.

Party Lines

In the headlights, fingers of fog weave
over the road, a seamstress just beginning
to patch together the loss of hours and years,

the maybe not and the not there yet.
I drive three hours to my mother's house,
arrive an hour later than she expects.

Still, she's waiting with dinner. She's
seventy something. I'm forty-six. We're still
mother and son. Before I'm finished with

the salad, she wants me to accompany her
to two parties this evening: a birthday
and a retirement. Between the roast beef

and mashed potatoes, it's all guilt. I continue
to say, "No," mentioning the chainsaw and splitting
wood for the stove, playing basketball with my son

and friends, and, of course, the drive, and in case
exhaustion isn't enough, I accept the label
of neglectful son, and whatever else she serves up.

Plato, Socrates' prize student, when he was eighty,
attended a pupil's wedding party,
and during the celebration retired

to a corner of the villa to sleep in a chair.
He stayed there until the all-night revelers
returned in the morning to wake him,

but he had slept too far into the Elysian fields,
leaving us with the question: Is it marriage
or a party that leads to the death of philosophy?

Troubled Water

From the ship's bridge, she captains the cushioned
recliner. The winded sheetrock walls tack and shutter
ever-so-slightly. Across the living room, she sails
toward an unknown destination. She refuses
to chart a course. Her friends think they know
and can see the shrouded shore, though no one is
certain if this is the place of a rich scented earth
and ripening fruit. A Columbus eager to plant
the flag and sword of the country she's leaving behind,
or is this just the story of every immigrant?

The wooden floor creaks as each step
balances on the next incoming wave.
Her face impish, as if only she knows
her secret port of call, she stares at the map
of a distant horizon. I only see the window
decorated with plastic flowers
and one living cactus that survives fitful
waterings of memory there behind
the impenetrable fog of heavily creased curtains.

I ask why she's watching the plaintiff
and the accused lay out their case of infidelity,
missing child support, back rent, unpaid loans,
stolen bike, as the camera pans Judge Judy's smirk,
her dismissive expressions, her ridicule
for such duplicity, without the sound turned on?
She says, "I know what they are saying,"
but she won't tell me, it's her secret.
Maybe she knows why we are sinking
into the murky waters of another afternoon.

So Much to Say

It's nine o'clock Sunday morning.
I pick up the receiver guessing
it's not a solicitation, non-profit or political,
or the phone company, but my mother.
She expresses surprise that she has reached me.
Wordless phone messages are her attempts
to call. She confuses the phone message
for someone answering. When she does leave
a message, it's all questions: "Is that you?
Where are you?" The answering machine
doesn't respond and runs until the silence
shuts it down. There's too much that we can no longer say.
We've screamed at each other before hanging up
or sometimes she begins the conversation by crying.

Leveraging

The house, an inflamed stillness.

Evening creases the curtains.
I don't dare to reach for the light switch.

No release
from the aching vastness.

Let a mother cry.

Beyond the window, the field
falls through falling snow.

The uncertain oaks draw
back in a blurred boundless ticking.

She offers the company
of the telephone book.

A depression glows as she picks
and polishes each chicken bone into a mirror.

Make a mother cry.

Her radio plays only martial music.
Her prophecies fill gas stations.

She won't forget those who danced
and died under a bomber's moon.

A man burns down his house
thawing frozen pipes, a woman lives

in ashes under the porch.
One tragedy rests in another.

The moon cries a mother.

Into the Wild

Everyday we go this far and no farther
then we step back.
We stare across the fence amazed
as bovine apparitions lumber across
the pasture, their wide wet noses
expelling all the world's air and then some.

*

We stare across the sidewalk at the wilds
of the curb, what has accumulated
during the night, so much lost or tossed
it's no longer possible to tell the difference.

*

We stare across the street believing
this must go somewhere and that some day
we can go there too, but not now,
not today, or tomorrow either,
we are simply not ready, unprepared at best,
and worse, to believe is all we know.

*

My mother now declares with certainty
from her bed in the rehab center
after breaking her femur,
that she owns two cars, one a Pontiac,
no doubt about that, the other a little more
indefinite, until I suggest a Mercedes pickup,
perhaps the red Mercedes that over the past year
she has paid for the title, for delivery, for inspection,
for a presale tune up, an undercarriage treatment.

Each payment followed with the promise
that it will be parked in her driveway in the morning.

*

$10,000 later she owns a decade-old Pontiac
Grand Am with high-performance tires
rated at 150 mph. The car will soon belong
to her grandson when I drive it mid-winter
to Portland. She will still have a Grand Am
and a red Mercedes parked in her memory.
She is happy just hearing the jingle of keys
as she lies in bed driving off to sleep.

Eating Crow

My daughter flies in from Seattle, my son from Colorado.
They think their grandmother is crazy and has been for years.
Manipulative. Delusional. Did they learn that from me?
My father, dead now thirty years, stood between us.

I don't want to drive to Kansas City and not just
because I've done it so many times recently.
After my last visit, she handed me five Western Union
"money grams" that had been sent to Jamaica.

Between October 10 and November 12,
they totaled $2200. My plan is to spread
these receipts on the table, ask her if she remembers
sending these. She will go blank, become suspicious,

unresponsive. She will not allow information
into her world that does not conform
to what she believes and what she believes
in is a red Mercedes. Cold, sunny day,

my son sleeps and his dog sleeps on the back seat.
My daughter studies for her anatomy
and physiology course: the complexities
of the digestive process, pepsins and hydrochloric acid,

bile and emulsifiers. I wonder how stress
upsets this chemistry. When we pull up
to the house, she's not there. I don't think
she would forget. She's always desperate

to see her grandchildren who are now 29
and 34 years old. Unfortunately, I know why
she's not here, though I don't say anything.
We discover the countertop stove is left on,

a cup of coffee sitting on the element.
A hardened black tar coats the inside of the cup.
The oven is on simmer with a large turkey
enthroned in an aluminum pan. Ten minutes later

she pulls her Grand Am into the garage.
The phone rings, the first of five phone calls
from the Jamaican car dealer. My daughter answers
the phone. I'm hoping they will confuse her

for my mother, but she doesn't understand her role.
The patois-accented man protests when told not
to call again. He claims my mother is his best friend.
My mother says they want to drive the candy red

Mercedes pickup over to the house so that I can drive
it home, and then they will return all the money
that she's sent. It doesn't matter what's said;
she can't hear how they are stealing from her.

The final phone call before we leave I answer
and pretend to be my mother. The man believes it.
My kids are laughing themselves out of their chairs.
He is pretending not to understand

why the truck has not arrived yet. He's going to find
out why and then call back. She has a stuffed turkey
fully cooked in the oven. How she managed to lift
such a heavy bird, stuff it, and sew it shut

for cooking, I don't know. My son and I
each hold a side of the pan and remove it
from the oven. The four us sit down
around the table and begin to eat.

How to Spell Muskogee

I.
She wants to know how to spell Muskogee, OK.
I ask her why and she repeats the question.
I spell the town's name and know that I need
to know more. Does a friend live there?
No answer. Is she buying something from there?
No answer. Is she requesting vacation information?
No answer. Is she a fan of Merle Haggard's
"Okie from Muskogee?"

Recently, I have called the police to ask for help
tracking down the Mercedes that has consumed
my mother's life. Each day she waits and expects
to see a red truck parked in her cracked concrete driveway.
A month after my call, a detective tells me
what their investigation has found out.

The people who call my mother are Jamaican,
but the money is not sent directly to that sunny,
marijuana besotted, befuddled island but to an old woman
in Muskogee, who suffers from dementia like my mother,
and according to the detective has no understanding
of what she is doing. The money is forwarded
to a storefront in Las Vegas.

The detective laments that they will never stop
the fraud or retrieve the money. But he's encouraged.
During the investigation, he is happy to report
that he busted three people working out of a trailer
who were "knee deep in stolen credit cards."
My mother never stops being helpful.

II.
My mother has remembered how to use
the telephone. No, I'm not Joe. I'm not Uté or Alice.
I listen and respond with half-appropriate answers.
Appropriate is beyond both our comprehensions.
It's been at least a year since her phone number
was changed a third time. There has been
no request for a money-gram in all these months
or the promise of a delivery. Nothing red
in the driveway except the ferocious tulips driving
fiercely up through the remnants of late snow.

She is calling this gray March afternoon to tell
all her friends that it is snowing though she only knows
one number to dial. The snow is white.
I try to imagine other colors including radiation.
She says the yard grass and the house roofs
are white. She doesn't know its depth; she hardly
ventures outside anymore. I tell her that it is snowing
here, too. She is surprised. She thought only her world
was turning white. We go through the checklist:
Is the dog fed and watered? Is she dressed?
Has she eaten breakfast, lunch, dinner?
What's the number to call in case of emergency:
211, 922, 119. What is she watching on TV?
I say goodbye, I'll call tomorrow, if she doesn't.
She says goodbye to Joe, says give your wife a kiss,
as my world is buried deeper in white.

III.
The hinges do not soprano
a stranger's entering.
She does not open the door.
The door has abandoned entering.
Meaningful and meaningless,
swinging open, swinging closed.
No transom for her to pass secrets.

There is the window
that she does not open and cannot close.
The window closed to itself.
So much in this house closed.
The screen and pane not cleaned
in years, so one filters and the other
refracts the anxious, tired light.

Then she points out where I stand
in the backyard, moving in
and behind the semi-circle
of spruce. *What do I find there?*
she wants to know. I want to know.
What day, what time?
My body abandons me
to this other investigation,
to not be there but to be seen there.

Stranger in a strange land lost in this distance
amid the circling spruce as their roots
weep stones upward into needle
and bark at the back of the backyard
where a fence declares limits
and the dissolving of her limits.
The chain-link has its own cross-hatched clarity,
draws conclusions that galvanize for a short time—
not to be there but succumb

to being seen there and finding nothing
that can be spoken or reported.

Rebirth

The floor dusted with baby powder,
sand scattered and smoothed in front of the door,
rug vacuumed so the ply pours only one direction,
the abandoned soul leaves no tracks
and always enters from the West.

*

The regalia of crow and heron feathers
his fringed leather jacket beaded red and yellow,
scintillating scales of light, jagged lightning bolts
slashed white and black along each arm and leg,
and a mummified hawk perched on a Sunday-bonnet,
ready to swoop down on the bodiless.
A thumb-sized crystal is strapped to his forehead,
beacon burning for moccasin quiet souls.

*

In the kitchen, there's admiration for the kitchen witch.
We sit on the porch swing recalling
a day that was all promise before
the breaking began. We float just below
the ceiling ready to circle the light
or beat up and down the closed windows
following the tiny torments of wasps and moths,
making up their instincts or making up their souls,
brooms already in flight through the room.

*

To defend their souls, the others know
two fingers are enough to make the sign
of the cross over their flayed flesh.

Third hand fingerless, bleeds on the floor,
reaching out for the already lost.
Two alleluias a binary proposition,
the third an unrequited echo. Tongues are sure
to tire and knot on anything more,
less a chance to lick a lie.

*

Only on Sundays—seven loaves are barely enough.
A forest of crutches by the door
are a sign of the liberated.
Who needs baptism when it rains each day?
Who needs prayer when the wind
never stops lipping the leaning house,
leaving endless rusting incantations,
until the mad soul comes running naked
out of the field convinced that its dreams
collide with the ravaged earth?
Castration and lopping off breasts,
eunuchs and savaged maidens of the new
heaven on earth, villagers turn to bloody
underwriters insuring profit on the time left.

*

To save their souls, the Hindu faces one way,
the Muslim the other. The Hindu writes
from left to right, and the Muslim from right
to left. Hindus pray to the rising sun,
and Muslims pray to the setting sun.
One eats with the right hand;
one eats with the left.
Who can remember?
Can anyone be sure?
Hindus worship cows. Muslims

are in paradise eating beef.
The soul stands in a soup line.

*

A busy day, the cat is in for emergency surgery,
this morning cutting and nailing boards
between floor joists so it can't happen again.
A busy week monitoring radiation levels,
civil wars, revolutions, while turning
the garden beds for early spring planting,
the snap peas are eager to wander through worms
and composted horse manure. A busy month,
decade, eon, but how could I ever catch up
with King David conquering Jerusalem,
his son, King Solomon, building the First Temple;
the Babylonian Nebuchadnezzar, conquering Jerusalem
again and destroying the First Temple; then the Persian
take over when the Judeans return to build
the Second Temple; then King Herod reconstructs
and expands what has fallen down, and less
than a century later the Romans take Jerusalem
and destroy the Second Temple, leaving
the Western Wall covered with the ancient dust
of conquest fine as baby powder over the soul.

II.

Instant Orphan

In the bank building's shadows, she pauses.
Late afternoon stretches its accents along the street.
Clouds park tight against the sky's blue curb.

Already working toward tomorrow, the pastry chef
kneads and pounds a hip of dough, rolls it flat,
pinches it closed, slides it into the oven of evening.

Just as she would do, ready to feed the hungry and forlorn,
as the sea breeze presses the flower print dress
that outlines her own never-to-be-satisfied hungers.

*

The birth certificate could be a forgery, its brittle yellow paper
mirrors the skin of my mother's forearms, hinting that it was left out
in the sun on a table in a room no one visited for decades.

It is dated close enough to the beginning of a war to be a kidnapping
or an adoption. Trafficking in souls, so many years later
she off-handedly says something about my other mother?

She can't say anything more, leaving it open to any stranger
on the street who could be something more, or less,
as she bends slightly to smooth the front of her dress.

Punch Line

Not quite after dinner, but after the *jägerschnitzel*
in burgundy sauce heavy with mushrooms,
noodle dish of *spätzle*, ending with *apfelstrudel*,
when the elderly woman crowned by her coiffed,
dark-dyed hair begins her story in her six-decades long
accented English. She wants to make it clear
how primitive the Russian army was when it overran
her town near Berlin at war's end. A soldier needed
to wash his only pair of socks. In the occupied house
that still had half its windows, the kitchen sink
didn't work, neither did the bath,
but there was water in the toilet where he dropped
his socks and began to agitate them. He accidentally
flushed his socks. His face reddened as he shouted,
"Those damn Germans even trained toilets to steal
from us." I didn't realize she was telling a joke.
It's how the defeated become victorious.
It's really not that funny. Maybe you had to be there
in the rubble and rape of it all.
In 1945, a clean pair of socks might have been worth
a man's life. The bootless corpse he'd passed, seated,
leaning against a sign post beside a cratered road,
the soldier thought, *Why does a dead man need
warm feet?* The beginning of another joke.

The Hungry

Over the phone most evenings, my mother tells me
she's cooked enough food for ten people: ham, roast,
always a chicken, with some assortment of side dishes,
sure to include overcooked canned green beans and iceberg lettuce.

I always ask who she expects to see at the table?
Who did she invite? Her answer, she can always find
hungry people, followed by the regular complaint,
when will I be there to help her eat this feast?

No one has shown up for a variety
of reasons: car won't start, flat tire, sick,
and my excuse is distance, 160 miles, one way.
She always acts surprised, sometimes asking

me where I live though I've lived in the same house
for 40 years, and then more astounded that a round trip
from my house to hers and back takes 6 hours. She wants
to know if I'm married yet, which is another 40 years to reconcile.

Tomorrow the distance will be the same but feel farther.
In her kitchen, fired in hell, every pot and pan
scorched, unidentifiable remnants of a battlefield:
handles half-melted, metal bottoms warped by heat,

the defeated history of her falling asleep while cooking.
The guest list grows longer by the day, so much food to feed
hungry battalions of ghosts. And there's the frozen pizza
baked in its box, waiting to be pulled from the oven.

The Cookie Crumbles

Book-ended by holidays, Christmas still ahead, my mother
would bake three types of cookies. The first a whipped
egg white with chocolate chips beat into the white froth

with a touch of vanilla and brown sugar dusted across
the top of each dollop. There was little substance to them
and with each bite they dissolved in my mouth almost before

I could swallow, creating a craving for more. The second
was more of a sugar cookie squeezed out of a hand-held cookie press.
They were always in the shape of an eight-petaled flower

and the center was strawberry jam that congealed with baking.
A bouquet of cookies set in a china bowl. The third, not really
a cookie, but filling the spaces between the cookies

in the serving bowl, were pecans halves rolled in egg whites
and cinnamon then baked; they were my favorite. I couldn't get enough.
I'd pick them out of the bowl when no one was looking until gone.

Girlfriends

Over the phone she blurts out that my girlfriend visited her again.
This morning I finally understand that she's calling the Social Services
case worker my girlfriend. It's meant to be an insult. It implies
a conspiracy, and in this case my mother is correct.

Prior to what I now realize is an accusation, she referred
to a woman who had graduated a year later than I did from
the local high school as my girlfriend. I assumed
this was just my mother's overbearing, intrusive nature.

This growing craziness is driving many of her friends away.
She wants to know why my wife never accompanies me
when I visit. I tell her there are too many animals
that need daily care at our house. That's not wholly untrue.

Currently we have eighteen cats and two dogs. We live
in the country and these stray animals have adopted us.
Then it's not wholly true either. Recently, she heard
that my wife and I sleep in separate beds. She's also a provocateur.

She calls every woman involved with her welfare my girlfriend.
Girlfriend is just another way to slander and reject the people
who are trying to help her. She does not want to believe
or accept that she needs help as our phone calls erupt into shouting.

Who, What, When, Where, Not Why

My mother wants to know where's my father. I sit in the living room
in a cushioned chair opposite her beside a two-foot high artificial
Christmas tree I retrieved from the attic. It is centered between
two white-wired, knee-high reindeer bristling with lights.

I don't know what to say. I'm not sure who she's talking to.
Last week she wanted to tell me about my other mother
but then stopped. Secrets are secrets. I wasn't sure
how to ask what she meant, perhaps a little afraid
of starting another life so late in my own,
this one unraveling fast enough.

Oddly insistent, she asks a third time, her way to dominate
and distract the conversation, which is me telling her
she has to accept help: vacuuming, mopping, laundry, someone
to take her grocery shopping and to the hair dresser,
ensuring her complaints are heard: the high cost of gasoline,
groceries, and how her red Mercedes hasn't been delivered.

I leave her with the implicit and not so implicit threat
of being moved out of her house, even as she insists
that she can take care of herself though she lay
in the bathroom three hours unable to get up
until the housekeeper arrived. I mention how she backed
the Grand Am out of the garage, left it idling
for three hours until a neighbor turned it off.

Finally, I tell her my father, her husband, is in Leavenworth
Military Cemetery, twenty-five years now, on a hill
overlooking the Kansas River and its broad floodplain,
protected by antique artillery aimed at vast horizons.

Migration

I stare at my mother when she asks where I live.
I wonder if she knows who I am,
but then I begin to wonder too
after she alludes to my other mother.

Sure I can name a few dozen birds summer
and winter: there were the triton-like claws
of turkeys in the snow on the driveway,
the raucous staccatto call of a pileated

woodpecker, the insistent chatter of nuthatches,
finches, and cardinals, deer hooves headed
to the next ridge, the neighbor's boot prints
where she walked the dog.

When the snow melts, there's no trace
of that walk, the birds riding
the wind, the steps in different directions.

A Longer Distant Call

On a rocky Pacific beach,
I watch gulls swirl and dive
for something floating
in the water—one more creature
that didn't survive the day.

Wind blowing over me, I lie
in the sand falling asleep.
No dissolving as the cell phone rings.

My mother was stopped
fifty miles from her Midwestern home,
confused, disoriented, asking directions.
An ambulance picked her up.
She was looking for the police station
to pay last week's speeding ticket
but was stopped by the highway patrol.
She says it isn't even safe to ask
for directions anymore.

Now she dreams driving.
She doesn't have a gun
and can only dream using it.
The sun slips into the uprising
sea-fog's pocket. Am I back
already? I didn't know I'd left.

Dead Dog

I want another chance with the half-retriever, half-husky,
knowing now it's not indestructible. The dog was semi-homeless
for seven years. With no one living in the rundown cabin
across the hollow, my wife and I walked or drove over
to feed the dog that was more attached to the house
than to anyone who ever lived there.

There was at least one winter spent walking down
a snow covered slope and up the other with dog food
and then returning home. We never quite trusted
the seventy-five pound dog, so much larger
than even our most overweight cats.

But I want to do it again. I did so much wrong
even after it moved in to our house. I can't ever
make it right for this dog killed by the local preacher's
hounds who lived a quarter mile away.
The preacher never apologized.

My mother's next-door-neighbor calls to tell me
that she came over after many weeks of not communicating
with them. She tells them that the former banker
who used to live across the street, turned state legislator,
died. Her neighbor says she was crying,
that he could hardly understand her.
Maybe she couldn't find her dentures.

He says, she is more incoherent than any time before.
I tell him that I will call as soon as we hang up.
Talking, she isn't any more confused than at other time recently.
She still knows what face to present. The help she doesn't want
is on the way. I have done so much wrong.

Old Friend

My mother wouldn't respond to frantic knocking,
wouldn't answer repeated phone calls.
She was found passed out on her recliner
in front of the television that could be heard
across the street when the door was opened.
She had a 104 degree temperature.

Probably lying there for sixteen hours.
None of her friends strong enough to help her
to the car. They called an ambulance.
At eleven that night, in a snow storm, I passed two
separate jack-knifed semis. Windshield slush
forced me to stop and clean the wipers.

The highway was quickly covered in four inches
of snow. Swirling chaotically, quarter-sized flakes
turned into chunks of blowing light.
One hundred sixty miles to the hospital.
She is diagnosed with pneumonia.

I leave her bedside at 3:30 am and spend
the night in my boyhood bedroom.
The next morning, the hospital bed raised,
she's alert. More than alert, she's been tricked
out of her house. She wants to know why
she's in the hospital and who put her there.

III.

Ring Leader

I'm yelling at my mother over the phone
the way she used to yell at me
fifty years ago in the kitchen
of another trailer, another house.

Wherever, whatever it was: something broken,
something not working,
something misplaced, it was
undeniable, without doubt, my fault.

Now she's caught me.
It's one of her final satisfactions,
that I'm no different from her as she enters
into a second childhood.

This is a bad movie, two senescent characters,
their hair anchor gray,
backlit by a window, battling
for territory that's disappearing fast

as Arctic ice, knowing there's
nothing to be gained, defeat
everywhere: the polar bear gone,
the Arctic fox gone, the seal gone.

Nothing to hide and everywhere
to hide it. She can't talk on the telephone
and cook without dishing up
blackened oatmeal. She can't talk

on the cordless without tripping
on the basement steps. She can't talk
on the phone as the television broadcasts
to the neighborhood whatever it is

she's watching. I've repeated three times,
what I've just said, each time increasing
the decibels of my voice, as I grip
the telephone like a pistol expecting

kickback. The shouting resumes.
She believes there's a conspiracy
to move her out of her house where she's lived
half-a-century, and I'm the ringleader.

Cardboard Palace

The brick ranch-style house sits halfway round
a cul-de-sac. The garage floor was once
so clean it was a dinner plate.
How can I find her in these badly taped
boxes stacked high on garage concrete
now dust-covered and leaf-littered?
Sides and tops bulge, the lids forced closed
but not closed enough. After fifty years,
stacks of the now unsettled
with nothing to stop them spilling
secrets into second hand stores:

the labeled crystal gossiping
their lead content, as if a warning,
the finely woven straw laundry hamper
crowded with elegant rags,
the antique beer steins, boxes of 1950s bowling
trophies, what remains of the sterling silverware
not stolen by housekeepers,
all these echoes reduced to boxes
waiting to be driven to other homes.

The silence that comes before the house is empty.
The silence that comes after the house is empty.
Both immeasurable. Both measured differently.
Not a customer service representative available to ask
for assistance, to challenge, to channel complaints
into the vast bureaucracy of time.

Paper Hopes

What must be saved, a stack of rubber-banded losing-
lottery tickets: Show-Me Doubler that promises an instant
$100,000 and doubling whatever else is scratched into revelation
with the edge of a penny; Sky's the Limit written
in little cloudy letters but it only reaches a sky worth $75,000;
I-70 Baseball, Jackpot 86, and the 100 Razzle-dazzle.
Forty-year-old canceled checks, car repair bills for cars
that are now antiques or more likely rusting scrap metal shipped
to China; J. C. Penney catalog bra order, mammogram and cholesterol
test results; assorted gas, water, sewer, and telephone bills;
tax forms signed by preparers she's outlived,
all boxed, taped closed, ready for salvage.

Manifest

This was how the West was won and I'm not even thinking
back a half-century to the movie, *How the West Was Won*,
starring an ensemble cast, including John "laconic" Wayne,
who later patriotically fought in the war movie *Green Beret*,
My Lai waiting around the bend in ambush. The helicopters
beating senseless the air, but those rice paddies are farther west,
then again, maybe not all that far west.

No, I'm just wondering about how and if the north northwest
or south southwest was won or maybe is still in the winning
stages. The compass needle infatuated with every passing bit
of iron, fancy or not, but the best directions are confused.
The rush west: uranium and gold mines,
oil and gas fracking, roughnecks riding high on fumes
while water faucets flare, cough gas,
caring for little more than manifest profits.

*

No, I was really considering the knotted, gnarled,
three-inch thick, foot-long branch with a worn gray
river stone glued at a strategic point so it sits stable
on the basement window sill of my mother's house.
It doesn't roll off before I move it to a box crowded
with bowling trophies and Reader's Digest
condensed books. So maybe it's really about how the West
was lost or maybe never found. The plastic deer
with the headlights look, its hooves glued into the wood,
that's supposed to be a rocky ridge with a couple
of tiny pine cones mounted at one end to suggest
a forested mountain beside the pointed pine knot
that rises a few inches above the other two faux trees.
I take a pewter figure from one of the trophies,
a woman taking a step in a knee-length skirt, her face smooth

as a fifties movie robot with one arm swinging forward,
other swinging back about to bring forward
the ball for release—this is how the West is won,
bowling over mountains, dreams of striking it rich,
and now the house, with all its flaws, cleaned out,
ready to be sold for half of what it was assessed.

Tony's Army

Her bed is elevated to look down at the photographs
and a small brown cookbook dated 1940
with her maiden name inscribed on the title page.
She wants to know where I found it, and I can't tell her
that I packed up the contents of her house, what was once
so familiar, leaded glass on end tables and window sills,
a few Hummel figures from the top shelf of the cabinet,
too many beer steins, a few odd paintings of odder origin,
preparing the rest for sale. I want to know but forget to ask
where she was when she used these recipes.
There is so little room left even as the house is emptied.

I hold up an 8 x 10 group wedding portrait,
the extended family standing on four tiers of risers
taken maybe 40 years ago. We are time travelers,
time narrowing our destinations, never quite quick enough
to stay ahead, no matter how quirky we are with our evasions.
I ask her to name each person and to start in the upper left corner.
The first man's name is Tony, short for Anthony. He's a cousin
I've sat beside, both of us holding beer steins, exchanging words
that neither of us understood, laughing as our hands shaped
the air into meaning. Separated by two women, Andrea
and Gabi, the next man is Tony too. When she is finished
naming all four tiers, there is an entire family of men
with the same first name.

I open the photo album and place it on her lap.
Each page is crowded with 2 x 2 inch black & white
snapshots from beyond half-a-century ago,
not a half-life ago but a whole life. On each page
the past is running to catch up with the future.
Hand-colored wedding photographs: the bouquets
hand-painted pink and yellow, smiles beyond smiles,
the relief real, the war ended amid smoke smeared by wind

rising from a wrecked plane, a fleet of half-disassembled bombers,
white sails sheeting the village lake, couples holding babies,
holding me, father and buddies holding stringers of trout,
snow and fog shrouding mountains and valleys,
hikers filling the day with wanderings.
I turn the page to a larger portrait of a young
uniformed man wearing his army field cap
cocked to one side, his lips and eyes set,
confident and certain that life is ahead, and my mother
points to him and says Tony. Then I know:
her oldest brother in a family of eleven siblings,
the one who disappeared near the end of the war.
That's what everyone does, disappears, eventually
whole families, and a few, for a while, never forget
until they too are found smiling from the pages
of an album, their names forgotten.

Powers of Suggestion

Maybe it's the jangle of a cash register in the background
ringing up Friday sales: beer, cigarettes, can of pork
& beans; it's dinner time. Her voice struggles
to find itself a place: any town,

street, state. She becomes separated
from her sentences, meanings drift
toward the horizon, terra firma
a thing of the already infirm past.

She's going to walk home from the gas station.
I ask how she found herself there?
She needs someone to pick her up.
From behind a gas pump, a voice tells

her that she is at the nurse's station.
I want to suggest that she top off her wheel chair
before driving it back to her room,
her home until December when Medicare

stops payment and she is evicted.
All she wants is her two dogs.
All she wants is her two cars.
She only had one of each.

When you're a Jet, you're a Jet all the way. . .

It's something about gangs running up and down
the hall. What did they look like?
How many were there?
Did they flash knives,
point guns, swing chains,
parse gang tattoos,
wear leather jackets and combat boots,
make bearded threats?

Down this hallway, lined with photos
of glamorous dead movie stars,
the usual suspects of these patient's dreams:
Humphrey Bogart, Lana Turner, Marilyn Monroe;
wrapped in baseball pennants teams
that have moved away.
No one is allowed to lock their door.

She was grabbed from behind,
an arm across her boobs.
She needs three policeman.
The man who grabbed her
is the nurse's boyfriend.
She says not to tell the nurse.
Tomorrow she plans to board
a cruise ship and then a plane
for Morocco. The French Resistance
can sort all this out.

Dog Train

The box car rattle of curtain rings rattle off along
the track across the ceiling. Clouds of thin plastic
fall to the floor. The upside down engine
works its way to the turn that divides the room,
the destination always the same, a room halved.
The engineer waves his lantern from the caboose,
waits for the bed to move, but it never does
though it raises and lowers, feet and head separately.
Only a single passenger comes and goes
as far as the dining room and back.

I have taken away her car, her house, her friends,
her dog, just so she can be closer to my own failings.
The only thing she misses is her dog.
Sunday I bring her a borrowed dog,
a walker tree-hound named Mavis that is nothing
like her pet that now lives with an elderly couple
with a similar white fluffy dog. My mother is oddly
satisfied. The second Sunday, my mother calls
Mavis by the name of her lost Isabelle,
her seven-year-long companion.
Isabelle could walk under Mavis' belly and never
touch it, except that half of Isabelle's life was always
vertical, frenetically jumping waist high.
Mavis, a.k.a. Isabelle, learns quickly to sit close,
be patient, let my mother pet her but she is far
too big to jump onto the bed.

There is a hint of Little Red Riding Hood's grandma,
when my mother observes how large Mavis'
paws are when her legs sprawl across her blanketed lap.
Mavis' floppy ears rise above my mother's gray head.
For two hours, she's comforted by her dog.
Mavis answers to Isabelle. Call one dog

by another name long enough and it will come
as train whistles then enters the station of her room.

Doppelganger

My mother wants to know if I know that my mother
is a chain smoker. I don't know whether to answer,
yes, no, really? In Room 106 A, where she's been
moved, discharged from the rehabilitation unit
for lack of progress, but really because she was near the end
of her insurance and there was a new patient that could be
moved in for three more overcharged months, she tells me
that my mother showed up at 1 a.m. smoking and wouldn't stop
until the small trash can under the sink was filled with butts.
Shrouded in a blue pall, she couldn't see the television
mounted on the wall. This is what my mother tells me
about my other mother. Repeating the story,
I ask for a name but it has gone up in smoke.

The New Facility

1. Buddha in the Road

Falling, her forehead left a baseball-sized hole
in the bathroom sheetrock. She went from
independent, to assisted living, to a fractured hip
and surgery, in six weeks. After three months
of rehab, I'm moving her into a long-term
skilled nursing facility near where I live.

Staring out the car window, it's the first time
in four months that my mother is not walled-in.
We are driving through a snowless winter
of leafless trees, barren fields.
Light skips through clouds,
its luminous legs step from one
field to another without leaving
a heel print as we will all do.

We pass the exit for Odessa.
My mother reads the town's name aloud.
I wonder if she remembers
seventy some years ago, so many starving,
so many frozen corpses, so near to where
she once lived. She wants to know
where we are going. I explain again
in miles and minutes. I don't know
where we are going. It's just more time
to live and die. Her back is bothering her.
She leans forward every few miles
indicating that I should rub
her lower spine.

She turns to me and asks
why I'm engaged to a six-year-old.

I don't know what to say.
She read it in the newspaper. She believes
this is why we are traveling so far, to escape
the publicity. The highway rough
before bridges over creeks and rivers.
The jostle and jolt cause her to grimace.
She turns to me, "What are you trying
to do, kill the road?"

2. After Hours

Yes, there's the ache of resurrecting
the body from the tangle of sheets,
the daily reclaiming of losses until
they can't be reclaimed but believing anyway.
My steady gait along these long halls,
yes, *just a visitor*, that's what I tell myself,
just a visitor.

The color-coded don't care: green, pink,
purple scrubs, they've heard it from others.
They know, and there's no doubt
that sometime a list will be printed,
where my name is penultimate, no matter
how strident my protests. It won't do any good
to tear down the desktop-printed welcome sign
with a frilled border of flowers that's taped
to the door of the semi-private room.

For now, I'm not thinking about it;
in fact, each time I contrive, confront, conflate,
confound, collude with the possibilities, I'm not quick
enough to miss the whitewash stroke of denial.
I tell myself that it's good to have negative thoughts,
no, better, it's joyous. Not to get too carried away,
at least there's a thought, no matter how dark,
decrepit, destitute, at least, there's a thought.

IV.

Later Picasso

In the windowless dining room where those needing
help are fed, the painting holds still
as so much else doesn't. Framed, the white table cloth
mirrors the moon. A pair of sparkling wine glasses

drink a chardonnay light. Three chairs sit empty.
Small roses bloom on top of a knee-high wall.
The restaurant's timber-framed door is closed.
Window planters are frothy with petunias.

The table sprouts a black umbrella. Evening
and night are folding into each other. The flat stones
await the spike of heels. The next painting is labeled
Tuscany but my mother says the scene

is outside Price Chopper, and the problem is getting
the potatoes and water into the basement. She suggests
I put the single slice of bread from her dinner into my pocket
to feed the horse in a pasture whose gate I can't find.

*

At lunch today she is an artist. The small box of tissues
form the foundation for her three-dimensional food pyramid.
Behind the times, the USDA has moved on to pie charts.
Her unspoken instructions: first, fold a paper napkin once

into a triangle, then smooth and refold it a couple more times
before placing it in the middle of her untouched plate of food.
She leaves the chemistry experiment at one corner
of her tray: sugar and cream mixed with cranberry juice

aswirl in a water glass of diluted coffee.
A milky swamp spreads across her plate.

Squash slices are arranged into fallen dominoes,
no longer a theory, one against the next until

reaching the edge of the tissue. Potato au gratin is
shaped lovingly with her arthritic fingers. She reaches
for her napkin on the floor. Thin slices of red pepper
are the mortar for small blocks of meatloaf

crowned with a blueberry muffin gazebo.
It's really not that unusual, the building of small
dinner-time cities before any of the other
ancient citizenry arrive to declare their allegiance.

Last Meal

The other woman who my mother sits with
at the table set with a thin vase of red and white
carnations, makes no attempt to sit upright
in her wheelchair. Her legs extend too far in front
of her to sit close to her plate, which makes little difference,
since she refuses to eat the pureed chicken salad floating
in a bowl and the fruit-infused lime jello.
She harshly stares at the two of us,
and spits out that she won't eat until we tell the truth.
So is it the truth of cut flowers dyed a deeper color,
flown in from Venezuela or southern Mexico,
or the truth of her sweatshop sewn clothes,
or the hormone-infused, GMO, nitrogen fertilized dinner,
that she wants to hear. What truth are we withholding?

Fades Away

It's thirty-five miles north to the birthday party.
Small dollops of snow hide in the shadow of fences
along the highway, an unfinished dessert
left to melt in the weedy bowls of ditches
that stretch miles. My mother sits in the seat
next to me, buckled in, fidgeting with the shoulder
harness. She settles for the strap to stretch under her arm.
We've just finished lunch with the German choir,
a group she once belonged to. This can't be
January, fields free of everything but brown earth
under the bright heel of sky as we drive
north to a different nursing home to sing
for another former member who is 99.

*

The flat screens in the community room are tuned
to a television evangelist, turned too loud
even for the hearing impaired. The interior décor
is dark, brooding, belonging to a past decade,
where others have to and still others want to forget.
Canes lean against chairs, walkers stand folded
against walls, the aging choir sits in a wide circle joking,
looking forward to coffee and sugar cookies.
My mother mouths fragments
of folksongs that come too quickly
for her to remember. I step into the next room
where the residents are listening. A man clinging
to his walker asks, *Where's the choir from?*
I sure like that music. I want to join
that congregation. The single accordion
plays "Mein Vater ist eine Wunder Mensch."
Soon it is time to leave for that other country.

*

Yesterday, I embraced my mother
as I never have before;
my arms hooked under her arms
to lift her out of the wheel chair,
her feet having lost all direction.
I wrestled her onto the car seat,
and later out of the car, to meet 20
of her friends at a restaurant.
The choir was on its way to the next town
and the *Sangfest*. I asked, *What did you do yesterday?*
she says, *I was very busy*
I mention her twenty friends,
and it's all astonishment and disbelief.
Then, she cries for the missing.

Invasion

They come from another planet,
work their way along the hall,
so slow in their progress they are more

leaving before they arrive, as if having found
what they conquered wanting,
as if moving backwards toward that point

where distance converges and disappears.
Minutes later they are closer,
the clatter of their walkers

mixing with the sinister shuffle of feet,
wheelchairs needing the walls to steer,
their pop-eyed alien faces visible now.

They beetle along in their 1950s sci-fi infestation,
the exterminator already dead, devoured,
and resurrected as one of them.

They have no memory of another life,
only this Stygian movement
where there might have been a choir

and chairs to sit in and listen
to what they have not heard before
and will never hear again.

Decent Hour

I wake at 4:30 am—can't fall back to sleep—
a Gordian thought knots my thinking—sword
too dull to hack free of it. It's the way my mother
slurs words at lunch. Later I call the charge nurse—
stop administering pain pills—ground up
and sprinkled over her breakfast cereal—
since she refuses all medicine.
It makes her sick—wheel bound—
head heavy—listing—face slurred
against the hallway wall above the handrail.

False dawn too bright for the thin shale
of eyelids, I will have to wait
for a decent hour—after a few birds
have discovered they've survived
the night—sing—remind the charge nurse—
my mother would rather struggle
than sleep these days away.

For the Taking

I arrived in time to remove the jewelry from the refrigerator,
though what jewelry remains is a sleight of hand—
ruby tomatoes, emerald cucumbers, opal parsnips,
their luster dulled by wrinkled weeks and mold,
but that's not what worries her. The joke about cold cash
only rekindles the complaint of no money,
reminds her of three thousand dollars that she hid
somewhere, maybe in the car and I'm to find it.
I confirm that the jewelry is cold cash now.

*

From her bed, in the room at the end of a long hallway,
she confesses to visiting my house last night,
walking both floors, the stairs not a problem,
wheelchair not in the picture. The messiness ghastly,
pervasive, persuasive, though the rooms were *well-combed*.
What exactly was groomed to perfection she won't say.

*

From the cafeteria, we move to the recreation area.
At a table, I half lean into a conversation where words
are nowhere to be found. The photo album is open
to pages of celebrations and parties, lederhosen
and dirndls, beer mugs, knee-high wool socks,
embroidered aprons and white-plumed hats,
smiles in formal rows, dancers caught mid-air
above their shadows in the zenith of a schulplattler,
sailboats, castles, onion-domed churches,
altars buried in the ornate, half-timbered facades
choking with flowering wooden window boxes,
gardens lined with gilded Romanesque statues,
parades celebrating the volunteer fire department,

the 650th anniversary of her hometown,
heavy work horses pulling 17th century carriages,
monuments and cemeteries, precipitous valleys and deep lakes,
and wings of an airliner slipping high above the cloud deck.
A year is written in the margins of a page: 1988.
Identical photographs begin to repeat two-three times
throughout the album—thirty-five years ago
it was already deep inside her—housekeepers stealing the jewelry,
repairmen taking the antique toys, Jamaican car
salesmen looking up her phone number—a life for the taking.

Christmas Cards

Autumn's blued door blows open.
Winter walks in.
Wind's hallway is crowded with nervous leaves.
Frost laces the stunted grass.
High chevrons of geese fly past.
Drought's anvil strikes daily,
iron-hard ground with no entrance,
no exit, no turning around, no coming back.
Seasonal wreckage of weeds scars the roadsides.

*

I walk through the coded glass doors.
She wants to know what happened last night?
Where did I go? I missed my wedding!
Something I miss every few weeks,
and wonder if and when I will ever catch up
with so many vows, and how to afford
so many gold rings.

Before I can ask, where the wedding
was held, who was the bride,
who was invited, how many dinner guests,
she wants to know what ever happened
to the man who washed up dead by the
creek, river, ocean, wedding?
Then she worries I left
the front door to her house open
that she last saw three years ago?

*

She has no list and reveals no names.
The Christmas cards sit on the activity table.

She turns a card in her hand, turns it back,
turns it over, folding then refolding,
a papery water tumbling through her fingers.

The feathered swirls of white against
a deep blue; the dove dissolves as it takes flight.
The card inside is blank.
Lost friends are lost again, and other friends
disappear without their knowing
even as I address the envelopes.

V.

Time Zones

I'm told my mother was moved to the observation table
in the dining room. She is being monitored. She has lost 12 pounds
in 6 weeks. When I visit she polishes her plate.

This evening I'm wrong. She pushes around pebbles of fried shrimp.
I'd do the same. She's given up spoons and knives; a fork is for stirring
coffee. She fingers a few ketchup soaked French fries into her mouth.

A red trail down her blouse, the napkin is never quite where it's needed,
mostly protecting the floor. Cubed vegetables are Legos
for constructing her next inedible house. I've sold the one she lived

in for fifty years. It pays her bills, but she doesn't know that
and doesn't ask about it. Even her beloved dog,
who now lives with her close friends, is lost to her.

The elderly woman across the dinner table wants to know how old I am.
"You must be about 20." We go back and forth until I pull from
my wallet a Medicare card. "You're so young!"

The woman says she retired when she was 45 then corrects herself, 32.
She sits crumpled in her wheel chair eating all her years away.
At the front desk, the nurse asks again for the name of a funeral home.

Betty Blues

Sunday Lunch:

Ain't got nothin' to eat.
She holds the bread pudding bowl,
taking another bite.

Ain't got nothin' to eat.
Her fork is lost in gravy
fishing for a slice of roast beef.

You got everything
and I got nothin'.
I got nothin' to eat.
Nothin' to eat at all.
Just throw me in a ditch.
Keep digging and digging.

Looks like you got something
good to eat.
Looks better than what I got.
Green beans, roll, mashed
potatoes, roast beef
I got nothin' to eat.

I got nothin'.
Just keep digging and digging
I ain't got nothin' to eat.

Roll me in the dirt.
I'm sick to my stomach.
I don't care. Throw me in the ditch.

Dinner Code:

6-6-3-0 out yonder.
6-3-3-0 onion and she's surprised
at her own discovery.
6-3-0-0 onion—I'm cold.
I'm not the boss as a chocolate chip cookie
is unwrapped and placed beside her plate.

Now I'm freezing. Help! Help!
With her fork she taps out a secret code.
That's all I know: 6-3-0-0 onion.
I'm cold. Help!

What's this? Her plate,
another discovery: broccoli-cheese
stuffed chicken and a hash brown casserole.

Boys are crazy. Got no sense.
Gotta get them outa here.
6-3-0-0 oh, O. They're making me sick.
I can't help it. I'm sick. Help.
They're coming into my stomach.
I'm sick. Amen.
I'm sick right in there.
I can't help it, they're sick.
I can't take care of them.
I'm sick everywhere.
S-e-e-c-k-Honey, I'm sick.
Get me out of here.
Get me out of sick.
S-e-e-c-k-sick, please, heck.

Drawing her hand back
from her tablemate's plate,
she licks her thin fingers.

They're freezing my cookies.
Kill me, I don't care.
I hope you're satisfied.
I have nothin'. Amen.
My mother would kill me dead.

Far Fields:

Shouts from down the hall:
Get on home. Can't wait forever.
Must be a mother calling in her kids
from the yard, from far fields,
out of the rug that is about to be vacuumed.

Milk is poured over the flattened
potatoes furrowed by fork tines
as if preparing a field for planting.
Half-exposed cherry tomatoes
like Turner's buoys warn of a narrow
channel through this milky river.

Shredded shoals of chicken flesh
to be avoided. What's left in the glass
is added to the coffee then the orange juice.
Another shout, *Stay away,* but it's too late
for all of us at the table.

Celestial Music

I stare so hard the air begins to crack.
My back-of-Marvel-comic-special-sale X-ray glasses fail me.
I see through nothing. Handfuls of flesh misplaced
on my mother's face as her head lolls to the left,
I wait to see her, but the narcotic of sleep
is all she wants now. Bob is here to make the afternoon
special. He stands beside the piano beside the altar
in the multipurpose room with a guitar strapped
to his chest as he adjusts the knobs on his small amplifier.
He strums a few chords as he announces that Willie Nelson
at 82 played at the Blue Note just last month though no one
wheeled in to listen knows the month or that the Blue Note is
a bar, and many wish they were 82 again. The concert begins
with Willie's song "On the Road Again." Oh, how the audience
wants to drive out of this place. Hands in her lap,
my mother's fingers fidget as if she might be playing along.
Between songs, Bob makes a few adjustments, moves
the music stand closer to read the lyrics more easily,
then plays a top-forty Beatles tune from fifty years ago.
All the songs are thirty years too young for this group.
The forties, give or take a decade, Tommy Dorsey, Lawrence Welk,
Bing Crosby, closer to their hearts. The silence
between songs brings a smattering of instinctive applause.

Course of Events

Separated by the lunch table,
separated by air groomed
to conform to rules and standards,
released into rooms according to schedules,
separated by chance and luck, or lack of luck,
the ambiguity to those seated at the table
makes little or no difference.

Doris chants, *I died, I died, I died,*
and from the other end of the table,
just-as-wrinkled and gray-haired, Mabel
asks, *When is your appointment? When
do the "I dieds" stop. If you don't shut up
I won't wheel you to the door.* Door to what,
the dining room? Door is suddenly ambiguous.

A few more laments of *I died*, and Mabel says,
Yes, I know you died, you stink.
Doris sticks a straw into the whip-cream-covered
German chocolate cake. She confesses to no one
in particular, *It's a pretty good day, I might go home soon.
I know I will.* Going home is suddenly ambiguous.

Two Is the Loneliest Number

On the fold-out tables that crowd even the hallways
sit wooden centerpiece pumpkins, sanded round,
painted a flat orange, vertical stripes of glued-on
sequins curve up to the stem, sold at Hobby Lobby,
made in China. Burnished with wet autumn colors,
the table cloth displays the scattered silhouettes
of maple leaves, caught in a snapshot of wind, their falling
suspended until the fraying edges overcome decorum.

In front of her, a paper plate holds all that is expected:
shredded turkey for a mouth that's lost its dentures,
green-bean casserole to gum, jellied cranberry,
mashed potatoes blanketed with gravy,
sweet potatoes wearing an elf cap of foamy marshmallow,
and slices of both pumpkin and pecan pie.
Her fingers work diligently; she folds, folds
and refolds, the tablecloth's hemmed edge.
She stares down into her lap, ignoring the food,
ignoring the growing commotion of guests,
ignoring the children that have just discovered
the excitement of their legs, and crying babies
who don't believe in tomorrow.

One six-year-old wears a neon turquoise t-shirt
that spells in pink letters UNDER ARMOR.
Now my mother folds her napkin into something
incomprehensible as the excitement
of nothing in particular swirls around her.
Loud men talk bow and arrow, 30-30,
waiting in the dawn, in the dusk, in the woods,
as my mother sits aging with her aging son,
saying nothing, maybe a slight nod of her head
or hand indicating some response to the smallest talk,
a mindless question, before she becomes

an architect, the tower of mashed potatoes
moated with gravy, the bloody cranberries smeared
on the puffy white walls, no hint of a truce.
Her name on the table reserving chairs
will always be followed by the number two.

Other to Others

She won't say anything more
but I ask again.
She stares off into the distance
of the dining room tangled
with wheelchairs and walkers.
I can't see her horizon
or the distance and how long it takes
to get there. Or maybe there is no
getting there. The horizon will rush up
at the moment she sees a sun
that doesn't set but turns purple
and black, deep as the bruises
on her forearms, if that's what they are,
and not the map of a secret geography,
displaying two ragged coasts that could be islands
that almost touch, one bruise nearly forearm long.
Pointing at the blotches, she says,
These are your sisters.
Does this have something to do
with the last good war?
Sisters? Sisters I've never known?
Are they still waiting to be rescued
on their separate beaches any afternoon?

Mother, Could You Please Tell Me Her Name.

A white bandage covers the back of my mother's hand.
The date is written across it, as if this skin tear is another
milestone that will take an uncertain lifetime to heal.

I ask what happened. All my mother says is, *Your sister*.
After my usual confusion, my rearranging what little I know,
I begin my awkward interrogation: date, place of birth,

favorite color, how many languages does she speak?
I swim across the usual gulf of silence. I'm left to imagine her.
Is she related to my "other" mother? Is she older or younger

than me? I decide that she's younger, after so many missing years,
I've already settled into being the wiser, compassionate,
patient older brother. She's somewhere on the West Coast

maybe between Los Angeles and Seattle or she retired in Oregon
between Lincoln and Pacific City. She loves the salty smell
and sound of the ocean, the way the sea stacks rise up abruptly

above the surf, hosting their own arks of stunted trees,
birds, and wildflowers. She thinks that she is like those
stone spires, alone, except for the gulls and seals

that occasionally come to perch and rest above the ceaseless
turmoil of wind and water. Daily, she sits on the beach
letting the waves erase her as a forearm of history reaches out.

VI.

War Zone

Mother, I don't know what to say
and, really, I've never known what to say.
It all seems so crazy and pathetic now,
you crying at the kitchen table in your house
that I could never call my home

though that's where I spent my high school
years, and not to be ungracious, it's not
the years themselves but the many times our words
were swamped and sank below hearing.
Perhaps it was too much to be shared,

my confession that I would leave for Canada
rather than be drafted to fight an immoral war,
as if a moral war exists. But that was the advice
offered on so many bumper stickers, printed in red,
white, and blue: *Love It Or Leave It.* There was so much

to cry over and you found it again and again, but that was
so long ago. Now you have stepped on the land mine of age,
and I don't know how to act or how to save you.
I don't know what to tell you or myself.
How many years have you sat in a wheelchair

after you broke your leg and refused physical therapy?
Now the doctor wants to amputate your left foot.
I'm not sure that you would understand.
There is still time to tell you, but tell you what,
that I've told the wound clinic no.

What good is a life without two feet,
even if you don't use them anymore.
We must hold on to the belief
that we can still walk away.

Rubicons

My mother, when asked by her nurse at the dining table
as I was halving tater tots with a fork and drowning the pieces
in ketchup before offering them to her, then quartering the meatballs
sans fluffy bun, if she knew my name, that I was her son,
said, "No," and "No."

Each visit, I cross the same bridge that stretches high over a muddy river,
the triangulation of massive steel girders welded and bolted,
buried deep in layers of paint, a trellised web that holds its victims
for maybe 30 seconds from falling into the churning water below,
before cars speed east or west, where the breath of morning
fog clings too long in the shadows of limestone bluffs,
damp gauzy night clothes draped over the palisade of cottonwoods
and bridge railings, over the concrete for all to see,
as the currents heave south to where another bridge
will wear a similar ensemble, until the temperature plummets
leaving a glaze of skidding and sliding, hurtling and hurled
against steel trestles and other cars, catapulted across lanes,
destinations lost, found, lost again, as traffic backs up ten miles
as collisions that take lifetimes to arrive are disentangled
and towed off after a few hours of cataloging losses.

The sky with its legions of shifting loyalties, squadrons of cumulus
and cirrus, tries out the panoply of possibilities, victory
as susceptible as defeat. The spring grass spreads
like a fever across these hills. Goats and cows follow
each easy mouthful across the slopes, as robins stop,
erect and alert, waiting for the movement of moist earth
to satisfy the next hunger, as ideograms of geese rewrite
the sky's slate stories, where my mother reaches
through the dinner fog amazed at the nothing she holds.

Final Observations at the Entrance to the Nursing Home

A distant lawnmower drones, on a mission to keep the grass
short and orderly. Back and forth, an army on parade,
booted and in lock-step, turns right to salute the empty
reviewing grandstand before falling below the blade.

Off and on, the thermostat set, the air conditioner compressor,
sitting on a concrete pad behind juniper bushes, insists
that it knows better and annoys everyone listening.

A mourning dove near the grain elevators coos,
who, who, so nothing is resolved though
everything is inevitable.

By the landscaped pool and waterfall, a stampede of water lilies
have left their round green footprints across the surface
where yellow and pink-petaled flowers not trampled,
glow, and below koi hover in that other world.

The figure of a straw-hatted plastic boy sits beside the pool,
the pants of his overalls rolled up to his knees, as if ready
to wade in, holding a fishing pole whose hookless line
never touches the water.

Three days ago she lost the use of her hands. Three days ago
she stopped eating. Three days ago sleep became
her last refuge. The water breaks over rocks,
folding and unfolding before rejoining the pool.

Purple Heart

In the charge nurse's office the mobile wound team,
on their weekly Monday visit, unwraps the bandages
around my mother's feet. The doctor says she's not
a candidate for surgery with such poor circulation.
(Surgery means amputation.)

Her feet have arrived from the trenches of WWI.
A rat has gnawed on the tip of her left big toe exposing
the bone (as if she lay abandoned in No Man's Land.).
Skin is discolored, necrotic, flushed red up to her ankle.
A piece of bone sticks to the bandage removed from her third toe.

The doctor recommends palliative care for gangrene and pain control.
(Translation: nothing can be done.) Shell-shocked, pain explodes,
as she tries to draw her feet back, her thin legs shaking,
as she folds deep into herself unable to cry out or even tear.
Nearly a century of wounds and now the sniper has a target.

Whistle Over the Top

A strand of saliva ties her lips together
though they remain parted and unmoving
as she inaudibly whispers, as her hand
weakly pushes my hand away. Is it a rebuff,
telling me I've never been helpful,
that I'm as useless now as I ever was?

I've always wanted to read my mother
a poem in her second language, in my first
and mostly only one. Children after WWII
were not taught the words of the enemy.
On her back for weeks, her bandaged foot
just changed, her toes in sunlight turning
toward night where no one can follow her steps,
no Orpheus to lead the way back, the promise
she may not remember and never made,
to always return to the darkness. I have
not read a single poem to her
though the morphine has left her listening.

The white-bearded gnome stands
on the windowsill, its overalls painted
the bright red of accidents, its right arm
embraces the stem of an giant sunflower
as if holding up a gospel of light,
eyes radiating, its face imploring heavenward,
boots so large that it will stand solid
no matter what happens.

As the body fails, the nurse removes
the bandages again. The toes are blackened along
with half the top of her foot. The nurse
says she can see through the joint
of the big toe, that it will most likely
fall off before she walks on.

Secret Protocol

On the radio, on billboards, I hear of clinics
and doctors advertising their therapies,
their promise of relief at last,
but I know there's little chance for me
and even if this is a denial of the possible,
much less the impossible,
the lost secret, a phantom limb
reaching to grasp the horizon,
the phantom pain more real than the loss.

Awakened on the cusp of revelation,
I can't remember
even what the secret hinted at,
only that it was momentous
and having not learned it
I will carry around the wound
of a missing life.

I didn't know her,
didn't know enough to ask,
didn't even look up into her face,
my head bowed maybe forever,
her face shrouded, her head hooded,
the moment's awe undared,
the distance unbridged,
the silence untouched,
the secrets unspeakable,
the horizon where she hides,
as the pages of war keep turning.

August 28, 2015

Friends of my mother told me about their recent visit
and lunch at the nursing home. Her longtime friend,
and like my mother is a post-WWII German immigrant
war bride, said that my mother didn't recognize her
or her husband. In fact, she didn't utter a word.
The friend paused, then said, the upside is
at least she didn't criticize us. At another lunch,
her first words to me, crisply spoken without
a moment's hesitation, before I even sat down,
were, GET A HAIRCUT. That was all she said that day.

In one of her kitchen cupboards, a white coffee cup
reads in large black letters: "You can tell a German
but you can't tell her much." The British philosopher
Alfred North Whitehead wrote, "All truths are half-truths."
I never knew how much to tell my mother,
what to wonder, what to ask, what is still true.

What was home for my mother, a citizen of two
continents, two countries, two cultures, two languages?
Was it hanging on the walls of her house, scenes
of mountains and snow-shrouded villages,
along with the plastic red-capped mushrooms
and hatted gnomes that crowded the floor,
window sills, and yard? The gnomes in the front yard
were regularly stolen. Was it half-a-century of living
surrounded by a spacious yard, hanging bird feeders,
the daily riot of sparrows and squirrels squabbling
over seeds, the deep afternoon shade of oaks
in the backyard? Tranquility was there for her
when she wasn't picking up every fallen leaf
and fretting over every stray weed.

Home is the accumulated stories that attend
a long life: her father on crutches, having lost
a leg in WWI, his ambling across the yard
scattering the ever-present chickens that roosted
in the barn half of the house; the decade
of hyperinflation when shoes were passed down
from sister to sister, brother to brother, socks
mended until there was nothing left of the original
wool; gleaning farmers' fields after the harvest,
hoping for a missed potato or handful of wheat;
knees and noses frozen riding horse-drawn sleighs
that worked their way through knee-deep snow
to school; and a fish dragged up the creek
from Waging am See, that was so large
it swallowed the imagination of the children
watching from the willow-lined banks.

She was born near a large and lovely lake
in the foothills of the Bavarian Alps, a few
kilometers from Salzburg, Austria. Her 1922
birth certificate was reissued in 1940, officially
stamped with the emblem of the Third Reich,
and I did ask her about that. She said,
"No one escapes history."

Same Two-Beat Story

The pasture darkens; only the starry glint
in a horse's large eyes can be seen slowly wandering
toward the horizon. Life, so abbreviated, Jupiter
and Venus, even the moon that unabashedly shares
only half its craters, is so far away, held by an ever-thinning
grasp of gravity. Unaware until it's too late,
we are unmoored and tumbling through our lives.

It's no surprise that Regulated Intramembrane Proteolysis,
also known as selective, or partially, or differentially,
permaneable membranes, yet with so many names
we still can't speak easily or directly, when the rate of passage
depends upon pressure, concentration, temperature,
all that we've considered at one time or another,
perhaps in different terms in our ever-flowing histories.

Or the Ramus Interventricularis Paraconalis,
more simply the branch of the right coronary artery,
an avenue lined with shop windows all tirelessly open,
telling and retelling the same two-beat story
until it's not, as if the cops have cornered another vagrant
to club into submission, and we are agog in space again.

Even the Restricted Isometry Property with its matrices
that are orthonormal when operating in the sparse vectors
of compressed sensing offer no stronger formulaic
guarantee to allow any of us to stand any longer
than we have, something I'm sure that we knew,
forgot, and we all know again, sooner or later.

How long does it take for us to discover, to accept
that there is no Relative Instruction-Pointer that's
worth any more than the next breath, no Routing
Information Protocol that will get us there and then
get us back, that we can possibly understand?

Or a Remote Imaging Protocol that will project us
back to where we were a moment ago
languishing in a final breath and then
the one before that reversing reductio absurdum,
so the claim that Recovery Is Possible
is hopelessly fanning infinity.

You never heard the Basque punk band RIP
from northern Spain or the thrash metal band
Coroner, or the song "Rust In Peace" by Megadeath,
or "Rock In Peace" by AC/DC that appears only
on their Australian album *Dirty Deeds Done Dirt Cheap*,
all so tiresome and pointless as if we need
a feedback-blasted, billy-club heavy beat
to defiantly accompany us when there's no turning back.

It's only the Latin, *Requiescat In Pace*, a dead language,
that saves us from saving us, the living, allowing us
the distance so when we are tumbling through space
we aren't in a mosh pit banging up against each other
asking whatever needs an answer and that is everything,
as the horse in the pasture opens its wings and takes flight.

Immortality

There was not a hint or a warning, so unexpected,
so unlike either of you. After 30 years, you're back.
At first, I didn't notice the mail on the kitchen table,
chaotic stacks of the opened and ignored,
the unopened and not thrown away yet,
their movement a supper ritual to make room
for fork and plate. The near endless stream
of advertisements, bills, the selling, begging,
demanding, never ready to accept that less
is more from a fixed income fixed upon less
and nothing. I notice an envelope addressed to
my father and an identical one addressed to me.
I open your letter first, an invitation to come
and listen, discover why it is so hard to hear
all that has passed, and the promise of so much
to be regained, resurrected, perhaps a whisper
that might carry you through the days to come,
or the song of a wren, though so many songbirds
are leaving us to face alone our own singed silence.
Yes, to hear the range, tones up and down the scale,
the last high and low note, and only to guess
at what is beyond the eardrum's pulsing beat,
even as I try to hear again the antelope-skinned drum,
found at the Goodwill, as it led my wedding procession
along the valley to the union of three creeks,
to hear again, the off key, the sharp and the flat,
and be grateful. I wonder if you are ready
to hear this, your last word a nod yes,
a weak squeeze of my hand, your lungs
swamped a third time, not to be drained again.

Even later, another envelope appears,
much larger and white, enough to think of snow drifting
over the hillside where you lie. You are offered a dollar bill,

attached to a letter, asking, requesting, no imploring
you to fill out a twenty-four page survey that will make
your opinion "count," make a difference,
but first you must be over eighteen, use no felt-tip pens,
pencils, or magic markers, only a black or blue ball point,
and make sure your "x" is centered in the square,
not in any way outside the box. So did you golf, fish, bowl, hike,
hunt, jog, or none of these in the last twelve months?
What about a zoo visit, a theme park, or circus, in the last year?
Where do you shop? How frequently do you attend movies?
A recent tanning or pedicure? How often do you vote?
How far do you drive to work and on what roads?
There's so much that needs to be known to make
your life better. Father, mother, when will you stop by to collect
your mail, so I can stop opening it and filling out your surveys?
What's the difference—that we are never finished, just done?

What to Say

   . . . walking on the roof of a spider web . . .
                    —Adonis

I will write mother,
I will write father,
but not yet, not now.
Soon, too soon,
only I will ask,
only I will listen,
only I will not know
what to say.

How much farther must I go
(go ahead write it) father?
Perhaps my (go ahead write it) mother
could answer that question
but not now, no matter
how hard I press my ear
into the dirt. My father's
had thirty years to cultivate
the wisdom of dust and silence,
the fleeting beauty,
and the endless whispering
of the grass; my mother only three.

*

The hand-written letter is six pages long
though only four are numbered,
the envelope cancelled—17, August, 1972—
forty-six years ago, nearly a lifetime ago,
pulled from a book pulled from a shelf
in the house's entry way,
The Blood of Adonis, by Ali Ahmed Said,
purchased the same day—17, August, 1972—

according to the receipt, the book unread
until now, though the letter was opened,
remained unread until now.

The first half was written by my father
in broad open stokes, beginning
Dear Son, and asking, *hoping
everything is fine,*
since the last time I called,
which was never often and now
not at all, but then maybe on my birthday
and maybe Christmas. I was lost to them,
lost in the world, wandering into the day
expecting nothing and finding
the impermanence that left me
curious and drifting into indifference.

*

I don't recall the package that you mention
with film for the camera and the shirt,
the book published by *Time and Life*,
though I do know with shaky confidence
that I've never read a Time/Life book.
Still I so want to say to you that I liked it
as you hoped. The cat just pushed the door open
and jumped on the keyboard sending her message
to you: 2323232323232323232323232323232323232323232323.
I don't know what it means: there are 24 "2s"
and 24 "3s" and they could be summed, calculated,
in many peculiar ways like our lives,
and still there is only one sum that matters,
the one that we could never add up together.

*

Yes, news from the neighborhood:
the Shield's boy has left for the Navy,
and Van Stein's son is army bound.
The Vietnam War has consumed so much.
Jane Van Stein has moved out of the house
and is renting a place in Independence
though you never mention divorce;
you are too polite for that.
The Oldsmobile is troubled;
the battery and points had to be replaced.
I don't remember if I ever wrote a thank you
to my grandparents for the birthday present
as you asked. What was it? I long to know.
Of course, we never escape the weather,
and for the last week and a half it's been too hot
and no rain. I don't know if the weather
was any cooler or if the relief of rain
preceded any rain of relief. As for the garden
and planting the seeds that I asked you to send,
all our lives are half-planted, half-cultivated,
half-erased before we know it.

I don't remember what was growing
in the poor soil behind the rented house.
If it's not half-erased than wholly erased.
Over the weekend you mention the football
game in the new Arrowhead Stadium
and a baseball game, the Royals taking on
the White Sox, the next day. The neighbor
across the street asked you to play tennis
but you don't have gym shoes.
So little and so much in the only letter
I ever received and didn't read until this late date.

*

Then my mother picks up the pen
at the bottom of the page, *Dearest Walter,*
and I stop: did I ever feel that dear?
There are still so many obstacles after forty-sixty
years. Her writing is more angled
as if in a hurry to get to the end of the line,
to the bottom of the page, off to some other life,
such as her friend wanting my phone number
to invite me to a dinner party, but I'm told the letter
won't arrive in time for me to send the number,
so my mother will offer another time.
Would that be alright.

Then there are the two packages again
and it's hard not to feel that I've lived an ungrateful
life. And, *How is work what a question*
to ask I must say. That wasn't very smart was it.
I don't know why. What was I doing at that time:
sitting at a desk in the Environmental Health
Center scouring census data or as a lab technician
in a physiology department caring for rats and bats.

And so it goes:
Did you like the color of the shirt in the package.
Did the bugs have fun with the garden.
Well how do you like that cabin. Is it nice to leave in.
And maybe that's what I've done,
after so many homes across two continents,
expecting to leave before I arrive: Mannheim,
Heidelberg, Waging am See, Bern, Neuchatel,
Charlotte, Hersey, Cincinnati, Kansas City, Columbia-
on to the next possibility as each day wanted
and waned. And a final question, written vertically
in the margins, *Have you been camping.*

*

Father, Mother, I refold the letter, slip it back
into the envelope, and notice the brackish-colored
stamp celebrating colonial craftsman, picturing
a glass blower leaning back with bulging, inflated
cheeks, as if playing a glass clarinet, then the wail
of silent notes heard over two centuries,
and that first class stamp only cost eight cents.

Archeology

Finally, I've dragged my suitcase up the steep stairs;
but, no, that's not how it happened, my daughter,
the labor and delivery nurse, has carried it up
the narrow stairwell lit mostly with shadows,
as if this is a squirming weight being born

into a world of attics. Satin blue body flat on its back,
armless, legless, more closely related to Frank Baum's
Wheelies in Oz, but without the threats and warning cries,
mouth a zipper that opens into its rectangular body
that cowered in the belly of a plane.

Crowded with contingencies that wait to be unpacked,
socks for tomorrow and tomorrow's tomorrow,
but the surprise is shattered. TSA, so kind to leave a note
in the shape of a book mark, tells me that I've been read
and even in my most desperate moments, I'm not desperate

enough. The inspector whose initials I can't decipher,
reshuffling my worn out secrets, did not rewrap
the 60-year-old Bavarian leaded crystal vase
that belonged to my mother, who at the end did
not care nor even remember it, but its many-faceted cuts

and glittering clarities, its heft suggesting something
of substance that should be passed from grandmother
to granddaughter, is now in a hundred pieces
and only a vacuum cleaner can gather it close
into slivers and shards of our ruin.

Epilogue

Exorcism of the First Spoon

The light entering through the window above the sink
inflates the room. The floor rises toward the ceiling.
The young boy stands on the kitchen counter looking down
at the immaculate porcelain, how it cradles the blue sponge
and gives rise to the monument of chrome faucets.
He sees the open drawer. Did he open it and step on
the folded towels or did he fly? The cabinets are before him.
The possibilities are far beyond what he knows.

This high the air is rarefied. Behind the first door are
crystal vases and bowls—this must be where the evil
ice king lives. The boy steals the king's wand.
The ice gods will avenge quickly but he will
overpower them with their own magic.
The second door is home to the wicked
Chinese emperor. He swings it open quickly,
grabs what he can, and slams it shut.
He's not turned into a spider. The third belongs
to the demonic magician. If the boy is to succeed,
he must slip between the floating motes of dust,
not touching a single particle in the cabal
of microscopic spies. He turns to see the red-faced
queen standing in the door. He gets down quickly.

The ice king, the Chinese emperor, the evil magician
are in pursuit, but they will have to wait their turn.
He forgot the simplest instrument in the drawer
beside the silverware and now he must place
his open hand down on the clean white counter,
the immensely cool white counter. His palm
feels the smooth grout between the tiles.
Love must be a spoon. Love must be
a wooden spoon. Love must be a broken
wooden spoon, broken across his knuckles.

Surely love is a river of broken spoons
flowing through every room, out the front
door, and down every street.

A Kind of Argument

She's folded into her wheelchair, head settling
deep into her shoulders, erasing her neck,
perched and waiting flight,
from Rome's Winged Victory to angelic
church icons hanging on candle smoke-stained
walls, hard eyes staring down for those
who pray to rise up, staring up at those already
walking on air. Her companions already
speak different languages. They only
have the long sentence of their stares left
to tell us, the wandering confused.

Behind her a door mourns open.
A dove pecks its way through
the mown grass. Her hands flock
over her lap, perhaps remembering
to shut the stove off that's on all day
and night, to remove all that burned
and charred, before she was moved,
removed from her kitchen, or is it
the steering wheel she's grasping,
recalling directions to turn right, left,
until she is balanced on a boulder
in the grocery parking lot, going nowhere.
I passed through you over half-a-century ago
and wonder how it felt and feels now
that you pass through me.

CPSIA information can be obtained
at www.ICGtesting.com
Printed in the USA
LVHW051504050819
626562LV00005B/839